The Heart and Soul of a Black Man

Featuring The Puppetmaster,
Carib-American Nubian Queen
and others…

By Warren G. Landrum, Jr.

Published by:
WarLand Books
2791 Explorador
Grand Prairie, TX 75054
warrenglandrum@hotmail.com

Warren Landrum, Publisher/Editorial Director
Yvonne Rose/Quality Press, Production Coordinator
Printed Page, Text Layout/Design
Madeline Haraway, Cover Design
Carol Landrum, Back cover photo

ALL RIGHTS RESERVED

No part of this book may be reproduced or transmitted in any form or by any means – electronic or mechanical, including photocopying, recording or by any information storage and retrieved system without written permission from the authors, except for the inclusion of brief quotations in a review.

The publication is designed to provide accurate and authoritative information in regard to the subject matter covered. It is sold with the understanding that the Publisher is not engaged in rendering legal, accounting or other professional services. If legal advice or other expert assistance is required, the services of a competent professional person should be sought.

WarLand Books are available at special discounts for bulk purchases, sales promotions, fundraising or educational purposes.

© Copyright 2006, 2012 by Warren Landrum and WarLand Books

Second Edition

ISBN : 978-0-9787355-2-4

Dedication

To my Dad, Warren G. Landrum, Sr.:
Taught me to fear no man and that no man is better than me— not even the President of the United States, because "That S.O.B. puts on his pants one leg at a time, just like me!"

To my Mama, Bynetta Landrum:
Showed and taught us unconditional love.

To my brother, Robert "Duke" Landrum:
Taught me to look at all people with tolerance and understanding and not to look down on people who are different.

To my sister, Dee:
Taught me restraint. If I had not learned this, I surely would have killed her at some point as we were growing up !!

I'd also like to dedicate *The Heart and Soul of a Black Man* **to my wife, Carol:**

Thank you….for being a positive stabilizing influence on me. I look forward to spending many more happy years with you.

The Heart and Soul of A Black Man

Contents

Dedication iii
Contents v
Introduction 1
Book I. Me 3
   A Statement of Me   4
   One Up   4
   Oceans and Clouds   5
   I Wonder   6
Book II. Special Inspirations 7
   The Puppetmaster (He's Everywhere)   8
   Carib-American Nubian Queen   10
Book III. Bitburg - "The Bush" 11
   Bitburg –   12
   Man on the Moon   13
   Emmy   14
Book IV. By Myself 16
   A Lonely Man   17
   ANNIVERSARY BLUES   18
Book V. On Blackness 20
   Black Christmas   21
   Yes, I Am A Black Man   22
   Twenty-Nine Days   25
Book VI. The Collegiate Years (The THOUGHTFUL Years) .. 28
   I am   29
   Freedom   30
   Truth?... Truth!   30
   To Mama & Daddy   31
   HAIR   31

MAMA	31
On Poets	32
The Opposite Of Sad	32
Awareness	33
Punctuation (To my Technical Report Writing Prof)	33
Musings	34

Book VII. The Love Boo 35k
A Letter To The Past (The First)	36
LOVE (The Second)	37
Moni	39
Ode To Kimmy Sue (The Third)	40

Book VIII. Smorgasbord 42
Little Island	43
Choc'late Sweet Thing	44

Book IX. For My Dad 45
My Old Man	46
Youngs town Sheet & Tube	47

Book X. The Hallmark Book 48
Here's To You	49
Easter Poem To Carol	49
Invitation To A Party	50

Book XI. Songs of Praise 51
Season Of Love	52
The Real Bottom Line	53
Aren't You Glad	55
Faith	56
He Is There	57

Book XII. Platinum Plus 58
Lest We Forget	59
Lest We Forget (The Men)	61

Book XIII. Home 62
    The Lake (As I See It)   63
    East Chicago   64
    Duke   65

Book XIV. A New Century 66
    2000   67
    2004   67
    2008   67
    2012   67

Book XV. "A New Beginning" 68
    For Carol   69

About the Poet… 71

ORDER FORM 72

Introduction

Warren G. Landrum, Jr. has had one poem, "The Lake (As I See It)", published in the *American Anthology of Poetry – 1983*. The first poems in this book were written while Warren was a student at Indiana University from 1974 – 1976; some were written in Germany while in the U.S. Air Force from 1977 –1979, and the chapter containing the gospel songs was written in 1988 1989. The featured poem, "The Puppetmaster", was written in 1994 while Warren was on assignment on the beautiful island nation of Bermuda, and one of the last chapters in the book, 'A New Century", was written in 2006 as was "Carib-American—Nubian Queen". The most recent piece, "Twenty-Nine", was written in 2012.

The Heart and Soul of A Black Man

Book I

Me

Hello. Let me begin by saying that to understand what a poet writes, one has to have some idea about how he thinks. The first three poems, writ ten within three months of each other in the winter of '77-'78, will hope fully give the reader some insights into the mind of this poet.

The first poem, simply for lack of a better title, will be referred to as "A Statement of Me" because that's what it is. The second is entitled "One Up" and the third, "Oceans and Clouds". If you can decipher the title of the third poem, it will give you an even better glimpse into the individual who is Warren George Landrum, Jr.

A Statement of Me

A complex yet simple individual am I
I was born to live
Yet I was born to die
Ever looking for Truth
My main question is Why
Not knowing The Answer
Shall I laugh or shall I cry?

One Up

Every thing I say or do makes perfect sense to me
But when I try to tell some folks, they just don't see
They say, "He's Strange, or Different"
But that puts me way ahead
'Cause there's not another Soul alive
That knows what's in my Head

Oceans and Clouds

Whichever way the Wind blows
There goeth I
Because I'm just a Free Spirit
On an everlasting High
Sometimes, I know, I seem Depressed
Sometimes I appear to be Blue
But if you'd think as much as I do
You'd appear the same way, too
But, appearances can be Deceiving
They often tell a Lie
I really AM a Free Spirit
On my never-ending High

The last poem in this section, 'I Wonder' was written in 2001 and originally published in my book, "Let's Go Home to Indiana Harbor – Reflections From Mid-town America", but I believe it belongs here as well because it is a part of Me...

I Wonder

5/17/01

Will any body care when I pass away
Will anyone cry or shed a tear for me
On That Day
And I wonder what on Earth
My Heavenly Ledger Book
Will Say
Did I make a Difference in Any Life
In Any Way?

Did I lift somebody Up
Did I make some body Smile
Did I spread a Little Sun shine
As I walked along Life's Miles

If not, it's not too late, I hope
I can start – right now – today
To make a difference
So that the world will know
I passed along This Way

Book II

Special Inspirations

The following poem was writ ten while I was on a contract assignment in Bermuda in 1994. I had been talking to a Bermudian who was also a musician/song writer. I don't remember what the conversation was all about, but I do remember that it was pretty deep and inspired me to write this poem.

The Puppetmaster
(He's Everywhere)

Dance, Puppet Dance
Dance, Puppet Dance

You move as though you're in a Trance
You cry because there is no Chance
No chance to ever really break the string
Of the Puppetmaster

The Puppetmaster pulls the strings
He's the one who makes you cry—and sing
He's the one who causes everything (My Sweet)
He's the Puppetmaster

You used to know him as 'The Man'
The man who always had The Plan
The plan to keep you under hand (and foot)
He's the Puppetmaster

Do you think your life belongs to you?
If you do, who's really fooling who?
You know he runs it thru and thru (oh yeah)
Does the Puppetmaster

He used to rule with whip and chain
He used to like to watch you hang
From the mighty oaks—'Strange Fruit', he would pro claim
Would the Puppetmaster

But now he rules in suit and tie
And gazes down from pent house high
As he counts his money that came by (your blood)
He's the Puppetmaster

With him, you never have to think
Just do your dance, and give a wink
He'll pull your strings and tell you where to go
Will the Puppetmaster

You know, the Puppetmaster's every where
You can't escape his mighty snare
Or would you even really dare—escape
From the Puppetmaster

Dance, Puppet Dance
Dance, Puppet Dance
Dance awhile before he cuts your string
Dance for Puppetmaster

The following poem was written in the Spring of 2006 and was inspired by my wife Carol.

Carib-American Nubian Queen

She Is
Carib-American
Nubian Queen

Exuding a Quiet Dignity
Rarely seen

Walking Proud
Standing Tall
A Majestic Beauty
Here for all
The World to see

Her Loving Face
Framed
Accentuated
By that
Jet-Black Mane

Her SPIRIT shines out
For All to See and Feel

A Spirit of LOVE
And JOY
And PEACE
And HOPE

Carib-American
Nubian Queen
She Is

Book III

Bitburg - "The Bush"

This is where many of the poems in this collection were writ ten. Bitburg Air Base, by the city of Bitburg (home of the Bitburger Brewery), in the Eifel Mountain Range, in the Federal Republic of Germany.

The Heart and Soul of A Black Man

Bitburg –

A Place unlike Any Other, Any where
But everyone should go there once,
Then they would learn to care
About the simple things in Life
The things we seldom think about
Have you ever missed a Golden Arch?
Stay awhile, you will, no doubt!

You'll miss
Things like strolling down a Sunlit Beach
With that Someone you really love
Or sharing orange ice cream cones
While the Sun stares from Above

You'll look for that Special Letter in the Mail box
Twice a day!
And you'll learn to thank The Lord
That you're Alive to see Today
Though these things may seem Trivial
Or even quite Absurd
They won't, My Friend
If you live up on The Mount that is…..
…BITBURG

Bitburg – "The Bush"

There was a lot of time for me to just sit back and think while I was in Bitburg. A lot of thinking is good for the mind, right? Or is it? This next poem has something to say about that.

Man on the Moon

Man on the Moon, Green Grass in June
Bio rhythms out of Phase
Tomorrows, Yesterdays, Todays
Always something to think about
Life is Strange, of this no doubt

Why are we here, in this Time, in this Place?
Why do we exist in the first damn place?
Why do I think about the things that I do?
What makes Me so different from each and Every You?

I don't know the Answers
I only guess, I think
Am I really very sane
Or am I on the brink
Of Insanity?

But then again, who is to say
What's Sane and what is not?
My Mind is merely ram bling now
It must be time to STOP !!!

The Heart and Soul of A Black Man

I met a girl while I was at Bitburg. Although we spoke two completely different languages, there passed between us the most natural feeling of warmth that I had ever experienced. This next poem endeavors to relate that feeling to you.

Emmy

I first saw her one Monday Eve
It was a quiet, Moon lit Night
To my Heart and to my Rest less Soul
It was Love at the very First Sight

Her Body, it was so petite
Her complexion—that of coffee with cream
I had to pinch myself at once
To be sure that she wasn't a dream

The most striking thing about this Lass
Was those Jet-Black piercing eyes
They penetrated the depths of my Soul
My Mind they hypnotized

I stared at her and she stared back
We stood there quite a while
And then to my wonder and my joy
Her face became a smile

I next saw her one Saturday Eve
There was no moon that night
I should have known this was a sign
That things wouldn't turn out right

Bitburg – "The Bush"

It was quite by surprise, this second time
I was on my way back home
I chanced to glance across the street
There she stood—so all alone

I started walking to Her
And She came towards me
Again our Eyes and Hearts embraced
The Love flowed so naturally

I held her hand and she held mine
For what seemed Forever and a Day
I knew at once, right then, some how
That my Emmy was going away

I know I'll never see her again
But I want to thank God above
For giving us just that little time
To share in Each Other's Love

Book IV

By Myself

At different times throughout our lives, we are alone. You can be with a crowd of people at a baseball game or on a heavily congested beach and still be as alone as if you were by yourself.

One can have all of the material things in the world, but if you don't have anyone to share them with, they really don't mean a thing. At the time I was writing these poems, I guess it must have appeared to people that really did not know me, as well as to some of my friends, that I had it made. I was in the Air Force in Germany and I had made a name for myself throughout the military community as a singer. I had one of the better jobs in the Air Force and quite a few friends. I was a BMOC—U.S. Air Force style.

By Myself

Even though I was the "Life of the Party", if people could have looked into my heart, this is what they would have seen….

A Lonely Man

Here I sit alone in my four-cornered room
My Eyes filled with tears
And my Heart filled with gloom
Is there Anyone or Any thing
Throughout this Land
That can ease the sorrows of a Lonely Man?

I've traveled and traveled
From Coast to Coast
I've been throughout the world
In more countries than most
But with all of my experience
I still can't under stand
Why I, of All People
Am such a Lonely Man

Every man needs a woman
This I sorely realize
Someone with whom to share his cares
Until the day he dies
I guess I'll just keep searching
And hope fully I can
Find someone to share my Dreams
And rid the World of a Lonely Man

The Heart and Soul of A Black Man

Loneliness also found me many years later and knocked on my door. I was in Bermuda in the middle of a 7-month work contract, as our 6th wedding anniversary approached...

ANNIVERSARY BLUES

7-21-94

With pen in hand
I send my love from me to you
As we approach another anniversary

I wish I could
Just touch my nose and be with you
As we approach another anniversary

My love grows strong
I'm wanting you when you're not here
As we approach another anniversary

My love grows deep
It's deeper than the ocean depths
As we approach another anniversary

I've got the blues
I'll never roam this far again
As we approach another anniversary

By Myself

I'll go to sleep
And that way it won't hurt so much
As we approach another anniversary

I'll see you soon
We'll hold each other tight again
And we'll recall that lonely anniversary

Book V

On Blackness

Too many times in the past, we have seen the word "Black" or the color Black, take on a negative connotation. The classic example that comes to mind is that of the American Western. We all know how to tell the 'Good Guys' from the 'Bad Guys'. It's by the color of their hats.

The 'Good Guys' always wore white hats and the 'Bad Guys' wore the black ones. What color did the Wicked Witch of the West wear? Black, of course! And what was the name of that infamous day when the Stock Market crashed in 1929? Black Monday!

These are all examples of the subtle form of brain washing that the American people have been subjected to for decades. It is not my wish here to get off into an in-depth discussion of this subject. My next poem simply offers one example of how the word 'Black' or the concept of Black can indeed be given a positive meaning.

Black Christmas

I'm dreaming of a Black Christ mas
Unlike the ones I've seen before
Let each Child be happy
Though his Head be Nappy
Where the Rich will truly help the Poor

I'm dreaming of a Black Christ mas
Where Understanding reigns through out
No more Hate or Sorrow
Just glad Tomorrows
Where All can Dance and Sing and Shout

I'm dreaming of a Black Christ mas
With every Christ mas Song I write
May your Dreams come true
And your problems be few
May you always see your Guiding Light

I'm dreaming of a Black Christ mas
For kids from one to ninety-three
May your days be Healthful and Glad
And may all your Christmases be Black

The Heart and Soul of A Black Man

The following piece was writ ten during the latter days of the Jimmy Carter presidency in either late 1979 or early 1980. It was a time when we had US troops in Cambodia. There was one commercial on television that they kept showing in which Rosalyn Carter (The First Lady) kept asking for contributions to help the starving in that country. For some reason with all the problems that we were having in our own country at the time, that just did not go down too well with me. Part of the next poem alludes to this.

The funny (NOT) thing is that it is now 2006, a quarter-century later, and we are still involved in a war over seas in a country where we are not welcome, wasting money that it seems could be better spent on solving problems at home, like maybe a National Health Care Plan, for example. Some things never change...

Yes, I Am A Black Man

And what does that mean?
I've been told that today I am a "Free Man"
Yes, I am Free

FREE –

One hundred and fifteen years after Lincoln
signed the Emancipation Proclamation

FREE –

Twenty-six years after
Brown v. the Board of Education

On Blackness

FREE –
Twenty-five years after one Black Woman
sat down to stand up for her rights

FREE –
Six teen years after LBJ and his
Civil Rights Bills

FREE –
Twelve years after the murder (I refuse to
Dignify it as an assassination) of King

FREE –
While there are still so-called American
Citizens running around in white sheets

AND YES, I AM FREE

FREE –
While many of my people are forced to
Choose between Heating and Eating

You know
I may be
A little slow
'Cause I've always failed to see
How worried we can be
About things across the Sea
When we can't take care of Home

The Heart and Soul of A Black Man

I mean
Can you believe
The President's wife
On TV talkin' 'bout
Toils and Strife
In Cambodia!!
When folks are struggling for Life
In the ghettos
Right here in the USA

I may be
A little slow
'Cause I fail to see
Why?

Yes, I am a Black Man
And I KNOW what it means
Do you?

I was commissioned by my church to write a poem for Black History Month in 2012. Since 2012 was a leap year, I decided to call the poem 'Twenty-Nine', for reasons which should now be readily apparent. Hope you like it…

Twenty-Nine Days

We have 29 days to tell our story this year
Of course this is impossible, Logistics apart
Not only because our history is ever-changing
But we really don't know where to start

Should we start back in the Bible days
With the Cushites, the descendants of Ham?
Or should we bring out the same old heroes and heroines
As we do each year, again?

Not that they don't deserve it though,
I'm sure you know some of the names

Malcolm and Martin and Mandela,
And The Greatest – Muham mad Ali
Or more recently Oprah or Denzel,
And Michelle Obama or Halle Berry

Or should we go back to Frederick Douglass
Or Booker T and Marcus G?
Or throw in a Sojourner or Harriet T
Or even George Washington C?

The Heart and Soul of A Black Man

But what about the everyday heroes
The ones that get no glory
I think it's about time we lift them up
And tell their various stories

Let's start it off with Big Mama
Who is raising her daughter's twins
While their 15-year old mother
Is busy getting pregnant – again

And what about that unsung hero – you know,
The one who gets no acclaim
I'm talking about that Father, that Dad,
That Brother who always has to be on his game

He works two jobs, and never com plains
He turns the other cheek when required
He does what is needed to provide for his family
And he seemingly never gets tired

Or what about that honor-roll kid,
That Nerd, That Book worm, That Geek
That College Kid who's in the Study Hall
While his peers are pledging 'Greek'

This is the kid who has no scholar ship,
No Athletic Pass or Full-Ride
Who has nothing but determination
And a little thing called Pride

He doesn't want to let his parents down
He's seen how hard they work,
He wants to show his little Brother and Sis
What Sacrifice can really be worth

So while we must not forget the past
We must also be aware of the present
We must constantly learn from each of these times
To ensure future prospects are pleas ant

'But Hey - we have a Black President now', you say
'So there's nothing we can't do'
But if you watch the TV and cable news,
You'll see, though this is true

Someone forgot to tell the Republicans
And some of our fellow Americans
Who are hating and dis respecting him
Just because of the color of his skin

Okay - 'Yes we can' and yes, we did
But unfortunately, our work is not done
If we want to pre serve what we have for our kids
It's up to every one

To exercise the right our fore fathers died for
And get out to the polls and vote
Vote against hatred, ignorance and greed
This may be our only hope

To make sure that when Black History Month
Comes back again next year
That when they start taking roll-call
There are still some Black Folks here

Book VI

The Collegiate Years (The THOUGHTFUL Years)

"...COLLEGE DAYS SWIFTLY PASS,
IMBUED WITH MEM'RIES FOND,
AND THE RECOLLECTION SLOWLY FADES AWAY..."

I'm sure that we all remember our college days (or maybe not, depending on your drug intake level ☺). And even those of us that did not go to college can remember those last teen years and the first years of "Adult hood". Those were, for me at least, days of soul-searching, questioning, thinking, and falling in Real Love for the first time. I opened this book with some lines from the Fraternal Hymn of my fraternity, Alpha Phi Alpha—because I still have some warm, very fond memories of that particular period of my life. The thoughts that I committed to paper at that time are reproduced below for your amusement. Most of them were written on the beautiful Indiana University campus in Bloomington, Indiana in 1975.

The Collegiate Years (The THOUGHTFUL Years)

I Am

I am What I am
And that's All that I am
No, I'm not Popeye the Sailor man

I
Am a Lover
Of all Things
That are Beautiful
To Me

Whether it be
Ice-Cold Kool-Aid
On a Hot Summer Day
Or a Simple Little Love Song
In Four-Part Harmony

I am
A Lover of All Things
That are Beautiful to Me
Whether it be me experiencing
Complete Love
Emotional Love
Physical Love
Love Love
With my Lady Love

I
Am a Lover
Of all Things
That are Beautiful
To Me

Freedom

(10-18-76)

Hey there, Black Man—Why so Sad?
You've been set Free twice
You should be Glad
Once in the 1860's and once in '64
If you play your cards right
You might get Free once more !

Truth?... Truth!

They say the Best Things in life are free
Be glad to be Alive
But it seems that THEY never really had
To struggle to Sur vive

I guess I'm glad to be Alive
I'm not ready to be Dead
But it would be so much better
If I could live without this Dread

The Collegiate Years (The THOUGHTFUL Years)

To Mama & Daddy

I never say I Love You
But I hope you know it's true
I wouldn't be writing this
If it weren't for You

I don't just love you 'cause I was
Born of, and raised by You
The Main Reason that I love You
Is 'cause You are always You

HAIR

What is Hair?
To answer fully
I must say it's
Black and Thick and Woolly

MAMA

Wise and Simple
Loving and Caring
Loving and Sharing
Beautiful, Beautiful

MAMA

On Poets

I've read poems by many poets
They use such big words, you see
If I were a poet, I'd make sure
Even kids could understand me

Their poems can be so very long
Sure, they're trying to tell a story
But what they must not realize is
That sometimes they are so boring

So I simply say what I have to say
And I let it go at that
And sometimes I don't even rhyme
But I did this time. How 'bout that?

The Opposite Of Sad

I'm glad that I'm Alive
I'm glad that I'm Healthy
I'm glad that I'm Black
I'm glad that I'm Me

The Collegiate Years (The THOUGHTFUL Years)

Awareness

There is a Man who's close to me
He's Close and Far Away
He's with me each and every night
And also every day

For one-score and two years, it seems
I've been pretty much in doubt
As to just what makes This Person tick
As to what He's all about

He's really unpredictable
Not many through Him can see
But at last I understand That Man
That Man, my Friends, is Me

Punctuation
(To my Technical Report Writing Prof)

Aren't you glad
That the world isn't Mad
Aren't you thankful
For Punctuation

Minus periods and commas
I'm sure there'd be traumas
In our daily communication?

I can imagine your faces
If 'tween words were nospaces
Now that would be
Quite a Sensation!
The End?

Musings

Have you ever wondered exactly
where you're going in your life?
Do you really know where you are?
Do you sometimes ask,
'Where'd I come from?'

Have you ever lay in bed wondering
just where it is you fit in?
Why did God put you here
In this time? In this place?
What is the Master Plan?

Sometimes I think that I
Have been here before.
Everything is vaguely familiar.
And yet—there's so much I do not know,
I could not have been, I think.

You know, I could die before I finish
writing the very next line.
So I will just thank God right now
For Blessing me so much
And I will rest my anxious Mind
for now.

Book VII

The Love Book

Three strikes, you're out! That's what they say in baseball. I hope it's not true of Love. The First Time, mine was unreturned. The Second was passion ate, beautiful, and meant to last forever. But, alas, 4500 miles and two years apart proved to be too much for even our feelings. The Third—well, the last poem in this section describes The Third.

A Letter To The Past
(The First)

May 7, 1980

I dreamed of You last night, you know
It's funny—I don't know why
You've very seldom crossed my mind
Since that day we said good bye

I thought I'd gotten You off my mind
I'd found a brand New Love
But I can't forget you'll always be
My First, though Unreturned Love

I know Love Songs aren't the thing today
But when I think of You
The words, they just keep comin' Girl
There's nothing I can do

No doubt You're probably married now
With a kid, or maybe two
But in my Heart, there'll always be
One place reserved for You

The next poem was written in two parts, nine years apart. The first seven verses were written a couple months after I met that beauteous creature and I was passionately consumed with her at the moment. The last verse was written nine years later with a tinge of regret and the thankfulness in knowing that my life was enriched, if just for a little while, with the presence of this woman in it.

LOVE
(The Second)

The first time we met, My Love and I
Was one hot summer after noon
I was busy playing cards, you see
When She stepped into the room

I chanced a glance—her Smiling Eyes
Were staring right at mine
I knew right then that we would be
Together in a very short time

She floated from the room then
Quickly vanishing from my sight
So I rejoined my poker game
Which lasted through the night

I asked and found out who She was
The next day I paid her a call
I knocked. She opened up the door
And said, 'Come on in you-all'

The Heart and Soul of A Black Man

I closed the door behind me
My Heart was all afire
We sat down on her queen-sized bed
And our Lips locked in desire

As her Mouth began to open
And her Sweet Tongue darted out
I thought I'd found The Answer
As to what Love was all about

Such a lovely, perfect Body
My eyes had never seen
And her Eyes—they had that sparkle
That was—um—oh so keen

Though that was nine long years ago
I remember it as yester day
Though it was short, I'll e'er be Blessed
'Cause She came along my way

The next poem is about the woman I just spoke of. Her name is….

Moni

(written from Germany while in the Air Force)
June 30, 1977

Her smile is so affection ate
Her voice—gentle and sweet
She's a bundle of Joy and Plea sure
To every one she meets

Like a Pearl within the ocean
The North Star in the Mid night Sky
This Lovely One called Moni
Is very pleasing to the eye

She's very real and down to earth
As to hang-ups, she has few
When asked who's Fairest of the Fair
The reply—'Moni is, that's who!'

The last poem in this section is about the Third Love of my life. It was particularly painful to write about, because at the time of this writing, unlike the others, I was still in love with her and knew it could never be.

Ode To Kimmy Sue (The Third)

This is an ode to Kimmy Sue,
Whose love I'll never share
This is an ode to Kimmy Sue
She of the dark brown hair

It was only yester year we met
For me—Love at the very first sight
She filled my dreams throughout the day
And danced in them at night

'Twas just my luck to fall in love
With a woman already taken
My enraptured heart was stole at once
My mind, seriously shaken

Beauty, charm, intelligence, wit
She lacks of naught—complete
But she's not mine
And thus my life is totally incomplete

Perhaps our lives will one day change
Perhaps fate will be kind
Perhaps through some strange twist of fate
Our lives and love will entwine

But until that day, I'll just go on
Searching throughout this land
To find a girl as good as she
And end the quest of a Lonely Man

Book VIII

Smorgasbord

Both of the pieces in this book were written while I was on a 7-month contract on the beautiful island of Bermuda. The first poem gives a little feel for what the island is all about. The second one is all about me being horny and visualizing my wife as a scrumptious, mouth-watering piece of hot chocolate dessert...

Smorgasbord

Little Island

(5-16-94)

Looking out across the Harbor
Watching as the Ships sail in
Night-Time Sounds outside my Window
Clip-Clop of the Hooves again

Orange and Yellow Stucco Buildings
Green and Purple, Red and Blue
Aqua-Green and Turquoise Ocean
Long Pink, Sandy Beaches too

From St. George's to The Dock yard
From Hamilton to Somerset
From Horse shoe Bay to Coney Island
From Spanish Point to Flatt's Inlet

Smell and Taste the Sea-Fish Chow der
Enjoy the taste of Swizzle Rum
Island Girls of Every Color
Make you very glad you've come

Hear the Soca – Reggae Music
Calypso Sounds and Rhythms too
Every thing that's New is Old there
All we need is ME and YOU !!

Choc'late Sweet Thing

Choc'late Sweet Thing
You make my Head Ring
You make my Heart Sing
You make my Body Ting
When I think of Your Inner Thing
Your Inner Juicy Thing
Your Inner Thang !

I count the hours till we become One
Till we come as One
And I get my Little Island Girl
Back in my Island World
And give her Head a Swirl
As we dance upon the Sandy Beach
The Sandy Beach !

Sexy, Choc'late Sweet Thing
I see you in my Dreams
I lick you up and down
And in and out, and out and in
And do it all again, again
And then I start all over then
From Head to Toe

Choc'late Sweet Thang
Do you know what I mean!?

Book IX

For My Dad

This book is dedicated to my father. He's gone now, having left us in February of 2003. In looking back, I realize how lucky I was to have one that cared as much for his kids as he cared for us. When I was growing up, he was my hero in spite of the many faults he had. I don't think that too many kids I know could have said that about their dads—but I could be wrong.

My Old Man

My Old Man is a Fisherman
If you ask me how I know
I lived with the man for eighteen years
So I KNOW that this is so

He first started taking me with him
When I was about five or six
But I was already more than ready
For him to teach me his fishing tricks

He'd come into my room at night
Maybe about one or two
He'd say, 'Boy, if you wanna go with me
You'd better put on your shoes'.

But I'd be way ahead of him
I'd heard him making plans to go
So I'd jump up—fully clothed you see—
And start heading for the door

I remember that first time like yester day
We went to the Kankakee Slough
That's where I caught my first—a Pike!
And became a Fisherman too.

For My Dad

Youngstown Sheet & Tube

Steel Dust in your too-black lungs
Shift work week to week
Union versus Company
More benefits you seek

Twenty-three years of Sweat and Smoke
Working on that tin-mill line
And there's only fifteen more to go
Before you've served your time

Yeah, fifteen long, long years to go
For that Gold Watch in your hand
And you'll hear them as you pass the gate
Say, 'Send the next man in!'

Book X

The Hallmark Book

I call this book my "HALLMARK" book. Included are a few verses that I wrote as personalized greeting cards.

Here's To You

Thinking of You across the Miles
Hoping every thing's OK
Wishing You some Xtra Happiness
On this Happy Valentine's Day

Praying that Your Body's healthy
And your Mind and Spirit, too
Once again, have a Happy Valentine's Day
With Love, from Me to You

Easter Poem To Carol

(3-23-89)

Christ died, and rose three days later
On that very First Easter Day
So I'm sending you these verses
In Remembrance of That Day

He gave his life because of Love
He died to forgive our sins
I write to You because of Love
A Love that knows no end

So, enjoy yourself this Easter Day
Eat a lot, but don't get fat
And remember, GOD and I both love You
It doesn't get any better than that !

Invitation To A Party

It's that Holiday time of year again
Time for Good Friends to get together
It's time to come in from the cold
And escape from the Wintry Weather

So bring along a Hearty Appetite
There'll be food to feed your face
Games and Good Music will also be there
Shake your booty all over the place

So come on over to Warren's Place
And let's party out the Ending Year
And don't be bashful—if you'd like
Bring along some Holiday Cheer

Book XI

Songs of Praise

This is a book of thanks and praise to God, who made possible all of my blessings, and gave me the strength, knowledge, and wisdom to be what I am today—whatever that is! All of the poems in this 'Songs of Praise' book, as the title suggests, were writ ten as songs of praise. I have already col lab o rated with a friend to put music to one of them, 'He is There'. If any of you musicians out there who are reading this, feel inspired to put music to any of the others, please con tact me at my e-mail address listed at the front of the book, and let's talk!

Season Of Love

A Positive Force is working on me
It's set My Mind and My Spirit free
I'm talking 'bout Love
The Love from within
That comes from the MASTER
'Cause HE is my friend

If you're wondering why
I'm flying so high
Just listen to this

All things happen for a reason
In a year, there's four sea sons
But in my life, for ever more will be
The Season of Love

As you walk along, life's Winding Road
Though Troubles may come, it's nice to know
You can share them with HIM
'Cause HE is your friend
He'll be with you always
Through thick and thin

If you want to know
Take my hand and we'll go
We'll journey together

All things happen for a reason
In a year, there's four sea sons
But in my life, for ever more will be
The Season of Love

Songs of Praise

The Real Bottom Line

All You ever think about is Money
Possessions and Worldly Things are on Your Mind
But I am here to tell you, it ain't funny
You better think about The Real Bottom Line

You say it's a dog-eat-dog world that we live in
And that's the excuse you use from time to time
But when the Final Roll is called
Will you be ready?
You better think about The Real Bottom Line

The Bottom Line!
You've got to treat your neighbor right, oh yeah
The Bottom Line!
You've got to learn to Love instead of Fight
The Bottom Line!
You've got to strive to walk in Jesus' steps
You better think about The Real Bottom Line

You scheme and plot and back stab all the day long
And wonder why you never have the time
Well this is all I got to say
You better take the time to Pray
You better think about The Real Bottom Line

The Bottom Line!
You've got to first learn to respect your self
The Bottom Line!
Before you learn to respect anyone else
The Bottom Line!
You've got to learn to Love to save your Soul
You better think about The Real Bottom Line

The Bottom Line!
You've got to treat your neighbor right, oh yeah
The Bottom Line!
You've got to learn to Love instead of Fight
The Bottom Line!
You've got to strive to walk in Jesus' steps
You better think about The Real Bottom Line

Songs of Praise

Aren't You Glad

Aren't you glad, I know that I'm Glad
Aren't you glad, I know that I'm Glad

I'm Alive and feeling OK
I'm able to shout and sing today
I'm so glad for JESUS CHRIST
Aren't you Glad

Have you counted Your Blessings today
I know that I count mine each and everyday

I'm Alive and feeling OK
I'm able to walk and talk and pray
I'm so glad for JESUS CHRIST
Aren't you Glad
Let's celebrate HIS coming today
Let's celebrate HIS coming today

If you have nothing to be thankful for
Then just walk on out the door
'Cause we are here to celebrate
HIS coming today

Faith

I've seen a lot of things in This Old Life time
And many a Long and Winding Road I've roamed
I've strayed from The Path at times
At times I've gotten out of line
But, as always, Faith has brought me back on Home

I've had my Ups and Downs in This Old Life time
No, Life hasn't always been so kind to me
I have screamed and I have shouted
But in HIM, I never doubted
And, as always, Faith has brought me back on Home

Faith is more than a word, you see
Faith is more than a word to me
It's knowing I'm never alone when times get hard
Yes, I've 'Kept the Faith, Baby', as they say
And that is why I'm here to say
My Faith is in the Power of The LORD

I may not be around for too much longer
But I don't care
'Cause there's one thing that I know
I'm back on The Righteous Path again
And that's why it don't matter when
My Faith has saved my place in My Heavenly Home

He Is There

In the Darkness of the Night
When nothing's going right
In your Deepest, Darkest, moments of Despair

HE will shine HIS light on you
HE will always see you through
When you need HIM
Christ the Lord is always there

HE is there thru thick and thin
HE is there when you want to give in
HE is there, my Brothers and Sisters, HE is there
HE is there for You and Me
And throughout Eternity
He'll be there for Me and You, yes he'll be there

When you need HIM, HE is there
When you want HIM, HE is there
Yes, HE heeds your every need—every desire
When you believe that HE can do
There is nothing You can't do
Just have Faith in HIM, HE'LL always be right there

Book XII

Platinum Plus

My church, the Church of the Disciple in DeSoto, Texas, named me as their 'Poet Laureate' in the Spring of 2011. The first thing that they commissioned me to do after that was to write something for their upcoming Platinum Plus Day. Platinum Plus was the tag that they gave to their seniors(50+). The following 2 tributes are what I came up with.

Lest We Forget

If they were a postal pack age
We would mark them as
FRAGILE – HANDLE WITH CARE…
And
Like a Fine Wine, they get better with Age

They were your Mother, your Auntie, Big Momma, your
Friend
These Silver-Haired Angels whom we hold so dear
They gave birth not only to our Flesh and Bones
But to our Hopes and Dreams as well
They taught us not to fear

They washed our Dirty Drawers
They nurtured us and chastised us
And
Yes, at times they even beat us
Because
We earned it!

But Yet
They loved us, they loved us, they loved us, they loved us
I said
They loved us, they loved us, they loved us, they loved us

They taught us 'Now I lay me down to sleep'
And they taught their daughters how to keep
A house hold… and a man as well

The Heart and Soul of A Black Man

In many instances along the way
There were two major roles they had to play
Mother and Father, Mommy and Daddy
So it's no wonder their hair has become so Grey

Now the collective wisdom that they have to impart
(If only we would listen)
Would empower our Spirits, give life to our Hearts

They have come a long way – from the Back of the Bus
To reign in our Hearts
These Women of Platinum Plus

Lest We Forget (The Men)

And what about these Mighty Men of God
These Silver Foxes
Who down a Long and Winding Road have trod?

Quick with a Firm Hand or an Encouraging Smile
They have done whatever is necessary
As they Inched forward mile-by-mile

They are Men of the generation of the Civil Rights Wars
And many of them proudly wear the Scars
Obtained some times by suffering or
Turning the Other Cheek
For Although they were as Strong as Steel
They had to feign as Weak

These Men of God are Awe some Warriors
And the fact that they still rise
To sing and shout and share their Stories
With a new generation of Boys who yearn to be men
Is an Awesome Testimony

'We Shall Overcome' was their fierce Battle-Cry
'I'm Black and I'm Proud' till the day I die
Young Men and Women, Heed their Voices
If in someone you must Trust
Of Course, God and Jesus lead the way
But then come the Men of Platinum Plus

Book XIII

Home

I finally left Germany and Europe and returned home after spending two of the most fascinating and interesting years of my life abroad. Home for me at that time (and I know now it will always be) was East Chicago, Indiana. East Chicago is a steel mill town that is located at the south western tip of Lake Michigan. You can look directly across the lake from one of the steel mills where I spent two summers working, and see the down town Chicago sky line twenty-seven miles away - that is, if the wind happens to be blowing hard enough to carry the orange pollution clouds out of your path.

I returned home and found myself sit ting on the rocks at the Lake one evening. Just as I was before I went overseas, I was awed by the huge ness of this Lake and its' raw, natural power. Maybe this next poem can help you to see it as I do.

The Lake (As I See It)

The Lake, it is so very big
The waves, they are so grey
It's a cool place to spend some extra time
on a Red-hot summer day

You can look as far as you can see
And You'll never see the End
You can enjoy its' serenity by your self
Or you can bring that Special Friend

You can sit upon the Sandy Beach
Or the huge, huge Rocks you'll find
You'll hear the sound of Waves on Rock
Just let your Mind unwind

Yes, there's nothing that's quite like this Lake
No matter where you may roam
It's Magical, Mystical Memory
Will always call you Home

The Heart and Soul of A Black Man

This is where it all started. Truly be it ever so humble, there's no place like…

East Chicago

East Chicago, not Chicago
Is the place that I call Home
It's the place where my Roots will always be
No matter where I roam

Steel Mills, Basketball, The Lake
Are some of the things it's got
Serbians, Mexicans, Blacks, and Poles
Thus the nickname, "The Melting Pot"

'Though I've been gone for many a year
The mem'ries will always stay
And I'm so glad I can always go Home
No matter how far I stray

My brother went into the hospital back home on the night of June 9th, 1991, the day after my sister Dee got married. He died the next day. This poem is for him.

Duke

Duke is gone now
But we're glad he was here
He filled every one he met
With Happiness and Cheer

They said he was retarded
But let me set the record straight
The ONLY thing he was lacking
Was the ability to hate

We were blessed with him for 33 years
Until the Summer of '91
The void I feel will never be filled
Until my days are done

I love you Duke
I miss you bro !

Book XIV
A New Century

2000
BUSH—Whacked !

2004
AGAIN !!

2008
A New Beginning ?
Or
The End ???

2012
Is President Obama
Our Man again?

Book XV

"A New Beginning"

"A New Beginning"

For Carol

When I think of the time that's meant to be
The time that's meant for You and Me
Our time is Now, Tomorrow, and Forever

Tho' we can't capture times that's passed us by
We can love each other till we die
Our time is Now, Tomorrow, and Forever

We've got a Lifetime, you see
We'll have the world at our feet
We'll walk along hand in hand
As we follow The Master's plan

Yes, the time has come to make One of Two
We'll make We and Us from Me and You
Our time is Now, Tomorrow, and Forever

Time has come to fulfill our Des tiny
Take my hands throughout Eternity
Our time is Now, Tomorrow, and Forever

We'll build a Life from Our Dreams
And no matter how hard it seems
We'll walk along hand in hand
Guided by The Master's plan

When I think of the time that's meant to be
The time that's meant for You and Me
Our time is Now, Tomorrow, and Forever

The Heart and Soul of A Black Man

About the Poet...

Warren G. Landrum, Jr. was born in East Chicago, Indiana on October 11, 1954. He lived there until he went to college at Purdue University, from which he graduated with a degree in Information Systems and Computer Programming.

Warren is also a member of Alpha Phi Alpha Fraternity, Inc., the first Black Greek- Letter Fraternity, established in 1906.

Warren served in the U.S. Air Force, both at home and abroad. It was while in the Air Force that he first became exposed to overseas travel, a passion that he would pursue at every opportunity throughout his life. While stationed in Germany, he was able to travel throughout Europe, experiencing the various cultures and lifestyles in Holland, Switzerland, France, Luxembourg, Belgium, and Great Britain.

Warren continued his traveling ways upon entering corporate America. He had remote assignments in Bermuda (7 months), Taiwan, Bangkok, Thai land (12 trips); and back to Europe again, this time experiencing Paris, Milan, Munich, and the London-Reading area. All of those experiences, along with his leisure/vacation travel to various parts of Mexico, Canada, The Bahamas, Jamaica and throughout the US, along with being married to a Jamaican wife, have truly given Warren a global perspective and insight in regards to both observing life and living life.!!

Warren and his beautiful wife Carol, are the parents of one daughter, Suzette.

ORDER FORM

Mail Checks or Money Orders to:
Warren Landrum
2791 Explorador, Grand Prairie, Texas 75054

Please send _____ copy(ies) of *The Heart & Soul of a Black Man* to:

Name: _____

Address: _____

City: _____

State: _____ Zip: _____

Tele phone: (_____)_____

Email: _____

I have enclosed $10.95, plus $4.00 ship ping per book for a Total: $____

Texas Orders:

Add 6.25% sales tax to total book cost for orders shipped.

To WarLand Books, 2791 Explorador, Grand Prairie, TX 75054

For Bulk or Whole sale Rates. Call: 682-351-6516
or E.Mail: warrenglandrum@hotmail.com

www.ingramcontent.com/pod-product-compliance
Lightning Source LLC
Chambersburg PA
CBHW050605300426
44112CB00013B/2085